This book belongs to
Daneil Kan

Written by Franzeska Ewart
Illustrated by Leonie Shearing

Language consultant: Betty Root

This edition published by Parragon in 2009

Parragon Publishing
Queen Street House
4 Queen Street
BATH BA1 1HE, UK

ISBN 978-1-4075-6855-3

Printed in China

Starting School

Franzeska Ewart Leonie Shearing

Bath · New York · Singapore · Hong Kong · Cologne · Delhi · Melbourne

On the FIRST school day, Sadie and her mom meet Sam and his dad.

"I'm excited," says Sadie, jumping up and down.
"I'm nervous," says Sam, holding Dad's hand tight.

Sadie's schoolbag has a picture of Cinderella on it. Sam's backpack has a picture of a soccer ball.

"I have juice," says Sadie. "And an apple."

"I have juice too," says Sam, "and an orange ... and cookies ... and chips."

Their teacher's name is Mrs. Bean. She comes to meet the children and says, "Hello!"

Sadie says "Bye!" to Mom. Sam says a very quiet "Bye!" to Dad. Mrs. Bean says "Bye!" too. Then she takes Sam and Sadie by the hand and in they go.

Mrs. Bean puts a sticky name tag on their sweaters. Above each name, there's a picture.

"Your cubby has the same picture on it," says Mrs. Bean.

"And so does your coat peg."

Sam puts his coat on the peg with the blue truck. Sadie puts hers on the one with the carrot.

Some children are already playing in the classroom. Sam wants to do a puzzle. He feels a little shy.

Sadie watches the other children. And in a cage in the corner, something watches Sadie ...

The children sit on the carpet by Mrs. Bean. Now she has the cage on her knee. From under some straw, a tiny pink nose wiggles at them.

"Do you know who our special classroom friend is?" asks Mrs. Bean.

The children raise their hands, but no one has the right answer. Mrs. Bean shakes her head.

"He's a gerbil, and his name is George," says Mrs. Bean. "And you've all got to look after him!"

George crawls out from under the straw and sits up.

Then the children sing a song together, to help learn each other's names.

By recess, Sadie knows Hannah's name.

Sam knows Ben's.

Everyone knows George's.

At recess, some big boys and girls come into the classroom.

"These are your Buddies," says Mrs. Bean. "They'll help you with your coats and jackets. And if you forget where the bathroom is, they'll help with that too."

Sadie is glad. She has forgotten already.

The playground is HUGE. There are games painted on the ground in bright colors.

The children eat their snacks. Sam gives a piece of orange to Ben, a cookie to Jessica, and some chips to Sadie.

They play hopscotch, and Joe trips over Sam.
Sadie helps them both up. The two boys smile at her.

In the classroom, Joe shows off his grazed knee. When everyone's admired it, Mrs. Bean puts a band-aid on it. She reads a story about a bear called Barney.

"Raise your hand if you know what color Barney's sweater is," she says.

Ben raises both hands and shouts "Red!"

"Good, Ben," says Mrs. Bean. "And next time, one hand will be fine."

The children paint pictures of Barney.

Sam gets a sticker that says: "I'm a star!"

He feels like a star.

On the SECOND school day,
Mrs. Bean plays a tape.

"It's Music and Movement," she says. "And first we have to warm up."

"Warm-up" is great!

step together.

Knee up high ...

reach up tall and ...

CLAP!

"I'm VERY warmed up!"
says Sadie.
Everyone is as red
as Barney's sweater!

Back in the classroom, the children write some words. At first, Sadie doesn't think she can.

Mrs. Bean writes a word with her magic teacher's pen. Then Sadie goes over the letters and writes "cat."

"Good job, Sadie!" says Mrs. Bean.

Next, they write some numbers. At first, Sam thinks it looks too hard.

Mrs. Bean writes the numbers with her magic pen. Sam goes over them. It's really easy.

At lunchtime, the Buddies come back to help the children wash their hands.

"Now find a place to sit down and eat your lunch," says Mrs. Bean. "And take your time. Only maybe not too long!" she says, smiling.

Sadie gets out her lunch. She has a cheese and salad sandwich, her favourite chips, a banana, an apple, and orange juice.

"Mmm! Yummy!" says Sadie.

On the THIRD school day, Mrs. Bean says, “I think George is a little smelly.”

So the children help her clean out George’s cage.

“On Friday,” she tells them, “one of you can take him home.”

Sadie hopes that it will be her!

"Today," says Mrs. Bean, "we're going to paint George."

Sam thinks George looks worried. (You can tell by his nose.)

"It's OK," Sam whispers. "We're only going to paint pictures of you."

"Roll up your sleeves!" says Mrs. Bean. She gives the children plastic aprons, and they start to paint.

"We'll hang the paintings on our clothesline to dry," Mrs. Bean says.

Mrs. Bean writes a story on Sadie's painting. Sadie can't wait to show it to Mom and Dad!

On the FOURTH school day, Mrs. Bean says, "Today we're going to have a teddy bears' picnic for all your bear friends."

"There's nothing to eat!" says Sam.

"You're going to make the cupcakes!" says Mrs. Bean. "And then you can add the icing ... and make faces on them, too!"

The children put on aprons and wash their hands. Then they make the cupcakes.

Mrs. Bean puts a name tag next to each cupcake.

"I know everyone's name," says Sam.
"Wow!" says Sadie. "That didn't take long!"

Then the children sit with the bears and eat their cakes. They sing a counting song.

Three little bears sitting in the forest ...

At the end of the FIFTH school day, lots of children get stickers.

"Now," says Mrs. Bean, "who's going to take George home?"

She smiles at Sadie. Mrs. Bean knows that Sadie would love to take George home. She gives Sadie a sticker that says: "I was a good friend." She hands her George's cage, too.

Sadie is so happy, she thinks she's going to BURST!

The children line up to go home.

“I like school,” says Sadie.
“I think I do too,” says Sam.

George wiggles his tiny nose. He knows he does!